A Note to Parents

Dorling Kindersley Readers is a compelling new program for beginning readers, designed in conjunction with leading literacy experts, including Dr. Linda Gambrell, President of the National Reading Conference and past board member of the International Reading Association.

Beautiful illustrations and superb full-color photographs combine with engaging, easy-to-read stories to offer a fresh approach to each subject in the series. Each *Dorling Kindersley Reader* is guaranteed to capture a child's interest while developing his or her reading skills, general knowledge, and love of reading.

The four levels of *Dorling Kindersley Readers* are aimed at different reading abilities, enabling you to choose the books that are exactly right for your child:

Level 1 – Beginning to read
Level 2 – Beginning to read alone
Level 3 – Reading alone
Level 4 – Proficient readers

The "normal" age at which a child begins to read can be anywhere from three to eight years old, so these levels are intended only as a general guideline.

No matter which level you select, you can be sure that you are helping your child learn to read, then read to learn!

Dorling **DK** Kindersley

LONDON, NEW YORK, SYDNEY, DELHI, PARIS,
MUNICH and JOHANNESBURG

Publisher Neal Porter
Editor Andrea Curley
Art Editor Tina Vaughan

Produced by the
Shoreline Publishing Group
Designer Helen Choy Whang

US Editor Regina Kahney
Reading Consultant
Linda Gambrell, Ph.D.

Produced in partnership with and
licensed by Major League
Baseball Properties, Inc.
Executive Vice President Timothy J. Brosnan
Director of Publishing and MLB Photos
Don Hintze

First American Edition, 2001
2 4 6 8 10 9 7 5 3 1
Published in the United States by DK Publishing, Inc.
95 Madison Avenue, New York, New York 10016

ISBN: 0-7894-7342-9 (PB)
ISBN: 0-7894-7343-7 (PLC)

Library of Congress Cataloging-in-Publication Data
Buckley, James Jr.
   Roberto Clemente/by James Buckley, Jr.—1st American ed.
   p. cm. —(Dorling Kindersley readers)
   ISBN 0-7894-7342 (pbk.)
   1. Clemente, Roberto, 1934-1972—Juvenile literature. 2. Baseball
players— Puerto Rico Biography—Juvenile literature. [1. Clemente,
Roberto, 1934-1972. 2. Baseball players. 3. Puerto Ricans—
Biography.] I. Title. II. Series.

GV865.C439 B83 2001
796.357'092—dc21
[B]   00-055542

Color reproduction by Colourscan, Singapore.
Printed and bound by L. Rex, China.
Photography and illustration credits
Andy Jurinko/Bill Goff, Inc.: 28; **AP/Wide World:** 4, 8, 10, 32, 42;
Baseball Hall of Fame: 14, 18; **Corbis/Bettmann:** 44, 45;
Dorling Kindersley: 8b, 10t, 42b; **Ebbets Field Flannels,
Seattle, WA:** 13; **Hillerich & Bradsby Co:** 23 ("Silver Slugger" is a
service trademark of H&B, Louisville, Ky.); **Major League Baseball
Photos:** 6, 7, 26, 32, 34, 36, 40, 46; **Pittsburgh Post-Gazette/2000**
(Reprinted with permission): 39; **Bill Purdom/Bill Goff, Inc.:** 16.

see our complete
catalogue at
www.dk.com

Contents

DORLING KINDERSLEY *READERS*

READING 3 ALONE

MAJOR LEAGUE BASEBALL™

ROBERTO CLEMENTE

Written by James Buckley, Jr.

A Dorling Kindersley Book

El béisbol

He ran like the wind. He had a cannon for a right arm. He was one of the best hitters of all time. And he was a hero to an entire country.

Roberto Clemente was born in Puerto Rico, an island in the Caribbean Sea.

He became one of the greatest rightfielders in baseball history. But to the people of his native land, Roberto was a symbol of how great they could be. His leadership and his caring were shining examples to all Puerto Ricans.

The sport he played is a huge part of Puerto Rican life. Hundreds of teams play baseball, called "el béisbol" in Spanish, all year-round.

Baseball is sometimes called "America's National Pastime." But in Latin American countries such as Puerto Rico, baseball is even bigger.

Many of these countries are poor. But that does not stop little boys from using milk cartons as mitts and broomsticks as bats. The baseballs are sometimes just old socks rolled up tight.

Roberto Clemente was the first great player to come from Latin America. Today, Major League Baseball is filled with talented players from the Caribbean and South America.

Would superstar players such as

Sammy Sosa, Juan Gonzalez, Pedro Martinez, Bernie Williams, and others have had success without Roberto Clemente? Maybe. Maybe not. One thing is for certain: Roberto Clemente was a

All-Star Bernie Williams

Super slugger Juan Gonzalez

pioneer for a part of the world that loves baseball.

This book tells the story of baseball hero Roberto Clemente, the young boy who was born poor in a little town in Puerto Rico...but grew up to make the whole world richer.

Puerto Rico

The island of Puerto Rico is located in the Caribbean Sea. It is a territory of the United States.

Miami, Florida
Puerto Rico
Cuba
Dominican Republic

"We played all day"

Roberto Clemente was born on August 18, 1934, in Carolina, Puerto Rico, the youngest of eight children.

Roberto's parents worked on a sugar cane farm. His father, Melchor, made only 45 cents a day, but somehow always managed to get his family what it needed. And what young Roberto needed was baseball.

"I loved baseball more than anything," he once said.

"We played all day and played until it was too dark to see."

Sweet stuff
Sugar is "refined," or made from a plant called sugar cane, which grows in tall stalks.

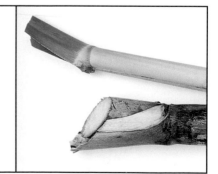

Kids in Puerto Rico played ball with whatever they had.

To earn money for his baseball
equipment, which was often not much
more than old tennis balls, Roberto
worked hard after school carrying milk
and other groceries.

Roberto was one of the best players in his neighborhood. He played on a softball team and used a bat made from a guava tree. His first glove was made from an old coffee sack.

He spent many afternoons watching pro baseball players in the Puerto Rico Winter League. Roberto became pals with one pro, a future Major League

Monte Irvin

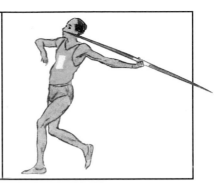

Strong arm
A javelin, long, thin, and spear-like, is thrown for distance and accuracy at track and field meets.

star first baseman named Monte Irvin. Irvin gave Roberto baseballs and tips about playing the sport he loved.

When Roberto was 14, his father gave him permission to play on a team sponsored by the Sello Rojo [SELL-oh ROH-ho] Rice Company. Roberto started at shortstop, but soon moved to the outfield to use his great arm.

In high school, Roberto also became one of the best javelin throwers in Puerto Rico. Throwing the javelin helped him develop a great throwing arm for baseball.

Everyone soon saw that Roberto was a special talent. The young star earned a tryout with a pro team called the Santurce Cangrejeros [kahn-gray-HARE-ose], or "Crabbers." Roberto had turned baseball from a hobby into a job. He earned $40 a week. When he joined, the team gave him a brand-new baseball glove.

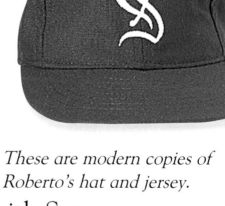

These are modern copies of Roberto's hat and jersey.

Roberto excelled with Santurce, whether at bat, in the field, or on the bases. His blazing speed made him a daring baserunner.

His many talents
caught the eye of Major League scouts.
Scouts travel the world looking for
players to add to their teams.

Several Major League teams wanted
Roberto to join them. But which one
would he pick?

Roberto signed with Brooklyn, but ended up in Pittsburgh.

At a tryout for Major League scouts when he was 17, Roberto put on an amazing display.

He fired the ball accurately from the outfield. He ran the 60-yard dash in 6.4 seconds; the world record was 6.1. And he hit with power to all fields.

The only problem was that the rules said he was too young. But the next year, when he turned 18, teams could offer him bonuses to join their team.

He accepted an offer of $10,000 from the Brooklyn Dodgers. But the next day, the Milwaukee Braves offered nearly three times that much.

Roberto talked to his family about what to do. They could use the money, of course, but Roberto had given his word to Brooklyn.

The kid who had started out with an old tennis ball and a tree branch was on his way to the Major Leagues!

Hello, Pittsburgh!

Roberto started on the road to the Majors with a season in the minor leagues. He played for the Montreal Royals, the Dodgers' top "farm team," for the 1954 season. But he didn't play very much.

Why not? He was a great player, wasn't he? But the Dodgers were trying to hide their young star from other teams. At the time, a rule said that if a team paid a player a bonus more than $4,000, he had to join the Major League team after one year.

If he didn't move up, any other team could claim him for themselves.

Since the Dodgers' outfield was full of great players, by "hiding" Roberto, they wanted to keep him from other teams.

But a player as great as Roberto couldn't be hidden. The Pittsburgh Pirates followed his career carefully. At the end of the 1954 season, they drafted him from the Dodgers.

Roberto played his first game for Pittsburgh to start the 1955 season. He never played for another team.

Back home in Puerto Rico, Roberto's family and friends were excited. Roberto was one of the first players from that country to play in the Majors.

He was a hero to many people there before he even played his first game in the Pirates' black and gold uniform.

Throughout his career, Roberto never forgot the kids back in his native country. "I send out 20,000 autographs a year," he said. "I feel proud when a kid asks for my autograph. I believe we owe something to the people who watch us."

But as big a hero as he was in Puerto Rico, fans in Pittsburgh wondered when this young star would live up to his talents. Several injuries and typical rookie struggles made Roberto's first few years very hard.

In fact, in his first five seasons in the Majors, he never drove in more than 60 runs in a season and batted above .300 only once.

In Roberto's sixth season, 1960, he blossomed. He led the National League with 19 assists. He batted .314, led the Pirates with 94 RBI, and was second on the team with 16 home runs.

More important, Roberto's skills helped the Pirates succeed. The team won the National League championship for the first time in 33 years.

The 1960 World Series was one of the most dramatic championship series ever played. The Pirates battled the mighty New York Yankees.

Roberto played very well in the Series. He batted .310 and had at least one hit in every game.

After six games, the Yankees had scored 46 runs and the Pirates 17. But each team had won three games!

In Game 7, the Pirates' Bill Mazeroski hit one of the most famous home runs in baseball history. He led off the bottom of the ninth inning with a homer that won the game and the Series!

Bill Mazeroski races home with the Series-winning run!

Roberto had a great season in 1960, and some thought he should be the Most Valuable Player. But he ended up only eighth in the voting. He was very disappointed to finish so low.

Orlando Cepeda joined Roberto in the Hall of Fame.

High average

Batting average equals the number of hits divided by the number of at-bats. Top hitters at each position win the Silver Slugger™.

But Roberto turned that disappointment into determination. He set out to prove the voters wrong. In 1961, he became the first Hispanic player to win the N.L. batting title with a .351 average. He would hit above .300 every season for the rest of his career.

After the 1961 season, Roberto and fellow Puerto Rican Orlando Cepeda, who had led the N.L. in homers and RBI, returned home. More than 20,000 people filled the streets on their way from the airport.

Not everyone in Puerto Rico knew who Roberto was. In 1963, he met a young woman at a drugstore and soon asked her on a date after getting permission from her parents.

But Vera Zabala didn't

Roberto with his wife Vera and sons at a game in 1971.

know that the young man who asked her out was a hero! She found out soon enough, and became Roberto's wife in 1964. Together, they would have three sons: Roberto, Jr., Luis, and Ricky.

Roberto continued to play well in the Major Leagues, frightening pitchers and keeping baserunners honest. He added another batting title in 1965.

After the disappointment he had felt in 1960 about the MVP voting, Roberto's success in the 1966 season was that much sweeter. He batted .317, slugged 29 homers, and knocked in 119 runs. And he was named the N.L.'s MVP...finally.

All-Star years

As Roberto continued to earn the praise of fans and players on the field, he was also earning a reputation as an athlete who cared about people.

He often gave offseason baseball clinics back home in Puerto Rico.

"Baseball is a great game," Roberto told the young players at the clinics. "The game can do a lot for you, but only when you give it all you can."

Helping others was a lifelong passion of Roberto's, behind only his wife and children and the sport of baseball.

"Anytime you have the opportunity to accomplish something for someone else, and you don't do it, you are wasting your time on this Earth," he once said.

Roberto certainly continued to help the Pirates. Though they were rarely contenders for the title, he remained among the league's best players. He won another batting title in 1967, and led the league in assists for a fifth time.

No player in Major League history has led his league in assists as many times as Roberto.

But even as he set records and amazed fans with his talents, Roberto battled against injuries and prejudice. As for the injuries, he had hurt his shoulder, back, neck, and elbow at various times in his career.

As for prejudice, Roberto was a dark-skinned Hispanic man in an America that was not always friendly to people of color.

Roberto climbs the wall at Wrigley Field to make a catch.

Early in his career, he had had to stay and eat in separate hotels and restaurants from his teammates. Even late in the 1960s, some places didn't want to serve Roberto and Vera.

Roberto, a Puerto Rican, sometimes received the same racist, second-rate treatment some black American players – and citizens – received.

Roberto did his part to try to change America's prejudiced ways. He played great on the field, of course, but more important, he demanded – and earned – respect off the field, too.

Along with his baseball clinics, he helped out in both Pittsburgh and back home in Puerto Rico. One year, he filmed an anti-drug commercial. He translated the script from English into Spanish himself.

He also helped younger Hispanic players, such as the Pirates' Panamanian catcher Manny Sanguillen, adjust to life in the big leagues. "I believe that every human being is equal," he once said in a speech. "But one has to fight hard to maintain that equality."

As the 1960s ended, Roberto knew there was more fighting to do, both on and off the field.

Highs and lows

The 1970 season was a special one for the Pirates and their fans. Their longtime home, Forbes Field,  closed in June. In July, they played their first game in Three Rivers Stadium.

On July 16, they honored their longtime star with "Roberto Clemente Night." The event was beamed by satellite back to Puerto Rico. Roberto's address to the crowd, in Spanish, moved many to tears.

Three rivers

The city of Pittsburgh is built around the meeting point of three rivers: the Monongahela, the Ohio, and the Allegheny.

His entire family was at his side as he received donations in his name for the Pittsburgh Children's Hospital.

Then it was back to baseball. The Pirates had surrounded their veteran star with a host of young talent.

The Pirates won the N.L. Eastern Division championship, as Roberto batted .352.

The Pirates lost to the Cincinnati Reds in the playoffs, but the team's success meant good things were ahead.

Roberto prepares to hit.

As the 1971 season began, Pittsburgh seemed in a position to make a run at the World Series. Along with Roberto, they boasted sluggers Willie Stargell

and Al Oliver and pitching aces Dock Ellis and Steve Blass.

Along with being a great team, the Pirates represented an important step for baseball. They were one of baseball's most ethnically rich teams. They often had lineups with more black players than white. And in a game in September, 1971, they fielded the first all-black lineup in the 100-year history of Major League Baseball.

Roberto was proud to be a part of it all. As he said in a 1970 speech, "We must all live together and work together, no matter what race or nationality."

The Pirates worked together well enough to earn another trip to the playoffs after the 1971 season.

Slugger Willie Stargell helped Roberto lead the Pirates.

Baseball playoffs

Today, the division winners and the second-place team with the best record earn spots in the league playoffs.

The Pirates faced the San Francisco Giants in the N.L. Championship Series. But Pittsburgh lost the first game. No problem, said Roberto.

"We will win this series and we will go to the World Series."

He and his teammates made his words stand up. Pittsburgh won the next three games to earn their first trip to the World Series since 1960. In the playoffs, Roberto hit .333, but first baseman Bob Robertson was the star, slugging four home runs and batting .438.

Next up for Pittsburgh: the American League champion Baltimore Orioles.

Although he was 37 years old and near the end of a glorious career, Roberto wanted one more time to shine.

He got it in the 1971 World Series.

Baltimore won the first two games, but the Pirates won the next three. Baltimore tied the Series by winning Game 6.

In a dramatic Game 7, Roberto gave the Pirates the lead with a home run. They added another run, and Blass held off the Orioles. The Pittsburgh Pirates were the World Series champions!

In the Series, Roberto batted .414 with two home runs and four RBI. He also had 15 putouts, and made an incredible throw to third base that Orioles catcher Andy Etchebarren called the best throw he had ever seen.

Clemente was named the World Series Most Valuable Player.

As he stood on the podium accepting his trophy, Roberto made history again.

He spoke to a worldwide television audience watching the game...in Spanish. He thanked his parents, and he asked for the continued support of his friends back home.

Star pitcher Nelson Briles with Roberto after 1960 Series.

With the cheers of the crowd still ringing in his ears, Roberto decided to come back for another season in 1972. Along with a chance at another World Series, he was shooting for an important milestone: 3,000 hits in his career.

At that time, only 10 players in baseball history had reached 3,000 hits. Roberto needed 118 hits to reach the magic number.

A players' strike and injuries cost him some games, but he reached 2,999 hits with three games left to play.

In a game on September 30, Roberto made history again.

He smacked a double to the left field wall off Mets pitcher Jon Matlack. It was Roberto's 3,000th hit. He was the

first player from Latin America to reach that important milestone. It was, sadly, the last hit of his lifetime.

After the Pirates lost to the Reds in the playoffs, Roberto headed home to Puerto Rico. On December 23, an earthquake struck Managua, the capital city of Nicaragua [neek-ah-RAHG-wa]. More than 7,000 people were killed, thousands more injured, and much of the city was leveled.

True to his nature, Roberto was among the first to help out. He called for Puerto Ricans to donate supplies and money to their Hispanic cousins. He worked around the clock to help.

Tons of food, medicine, and supplies were gathered and sent to Nicaragua. Soon Roberto learned that some of the supplies were being stolen. He decided to go there himself to make sure the people got the help they needed.

Earthquakes can cause terrible damage to cities.

On December 31, 1972, just three months after his historic 3,000th hit, Roberto climbed aboard a plane filled with supplies bound for Nicaragua.

The plane on the mission of mercy never made it to Nicaragua.

At 9:23 p.m., the plane carrying Roberto, four other men, and tons of supplies crashed into the Atlantic Ocean shortly after taking off. There were no survivors.

All of Puerto Rico, all of baseball, and all of the sports world were shocked by the sudden death of their hero.

No one was surprised that he gave his life helping others. But everyone was saddened to lose such a great man at such a young age.

"He had about him a touch of royalty," said baseball commissioner Bowie Kuhn.

But while Roberto had died, his contributions to baseball and to Puerto Rico continue even today.

Divers worked to try to recover Roberto and the others.

Roberto's legacy

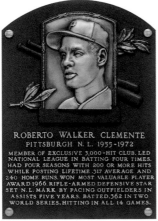

ROBERTO WALKER CLEMENTE
PITTSBURGH N. L. 1955-1972
MEMBER OF EXCLUSIVE 3,000-HIT CLUB. LED
NATIONAL LEAGUE IN BATTING FOUR TIMES.
HAD FOUR SEASONS WITH 200 OR MORE HITS
WHILE POSTING LIFETIME .317 AVERAGE AND
240 HOME RUNS. WON MOST VALUABLE PLAYER
AWARD 1966. RIFLE-ARMED DEFENSIVE STAR
SET N.L. MARK BY PACING OUTFIELDERS IN
ASSISTS FIVE YEARS. BATTED .362 IN TWO
WORLD SERIES, HITTING IN ALL 14 GAMES.

Hall of Fame plaque

A legacy is what people leave behind after they die. The legacy of Roberto Clemente is enormous.

Only days after his tragic death, he was elected to the Baseball Hall of Fame, the first Latin player in the Hall.

Today, Major League Baseball honors him each year with the Roberto Clemente Award, given to a player who combines talent on the field with community service.

One recent winner was Sammy Sosa of the Chicago Cubs.

In Puerto Rico, thousands of children enjoy sports facilities that Roberto never had as a kid at Roberto Clemente Sports City, near San Juan.

U.S. postage stamp, issued in 2000

Also, two hospitals in Puerto Rico bear his name, while schools in the United States are named for him. The city of Pittsburgh named a bridge after him.

Outside Three Rivers Stadium stands a statue of Roberto Clemente. Next time you see it, tell him thanks for everything he did... for baseball and for his people.

Still hitting: Roberto's statue keeps looking to the future.

GREAT ONE"

Glossary

Assist
The player who throws the ball to a player who makes a putout receives an assist; for instance, if Roberto throws a ball to the second baseman, who tags a runner, Roberto gets an assist.

Autograph
A person's signature, in this case a baseball player's.

Batting average
A measure of success for hitters; figured by dividing hits by at-bats.

Bonus
Money given to young players to convince them to join a Major League team.

Clemente Award
An annual award given to a player who is great on the field and in the community.

Hall of Fame
Located in Cooperstown, New York, this building houses baseball history and honors its greatest players.

Latin America
The Spanish-speaking area south of the U.S.

Minor leagues
Lower levels of pro baseball.

Legacy
What a person leaves behind after he or she dies.

Plaque [PLACK]
A flat metal or wooden shape that is used to remember an important person or event.

Playoffs
Games played after the regular season to determine a champion.

Prejudice
When people believe something about someone based only on the color of their skin or where they're from.

Putout
Given to a player who tags a baserunner out or steps on a base to get a runner out.

Scout
People who look around the world for new players for Major League teams.

Rookie
A player in the first year of his pro sports career.

Strike
In this case, strike means when workers stop working to protest something.

World Series
The postseason championship of Major League Baseball.